A Grayscale Martyrdom

poems by

Alec Montalvo

Finishing Line Press
Georgetown, Kentucky

A Grayscale Martyrdom

ACKNOWLEDGMENTS

"Casket Parts Hereafter" *The Esthetic Apostle.* October 2020. Originally
Titled "Casket Parts"
"Hole" *The Penmen Review.* January 2020. Originally titled "Mulch Mound"
"My Father's Heirlooms" *Gravitas.* January 2020
"Passersby in the Trainyard" *Inkwell Journal.* Issue 35

Publisher: Leah Huete de Maines
Editor: Christen Kincaid
Cover Art: Jane Saitova
Author Photo: Jane Saitova
Cover Design: Elizabeth Maines McCleavy

Order online: www.finishinglinepress.com
also available on amazon.com

Author inquiries and mail orders:
Finishing Line Press
PO Box 1626
Georgetown, Kentucky 40324
USA

Table of Contents

A Grayscale Martyrdom—
/'grāskāl/ /'märdərdəm/

1. A dispassionate sacrifice or one that you don't believe in
2. A display of feigned or exaggerated suffering that fails to obtain sympathy

Three of Swords

I have just finished the dig
in the yard
on my hands and knees,
dragged my heels in circles
around the pit as a ritual.

The canopy had collapsed
into white cloths mangled
with mud.

Shapeless wedding ornaments
buried, bumped,
wrinkled
across the grassline.

At night, they rise as reanimated bones

splitting through the wood.

I want them to remain underground,
work the system of soil
ghosting moons.

There's too little snow today.
It dusts blades of grass,
powders lavender,
levels the yard into even white.

But I was told your prints track you
in a timed release.

My hands can
bubble out the ground
the way rain clouds could
brim from your mouth

or berries bled
from your grip

all while the snow
keeps falling
on wood and bone.

Etiquette for a Dead Gamble

I am the tousled body bag
dragged
by mid island wind
like grocery carts
and ghost drivers
left out in empty
parking lots.

Feels like a bombardment
of guardrail reflectors
dimmed down in every
direction.
So lightless.

Tonight,
someone must
have screwdrivered
the mirrors out
on the side
of the embankment,
fashioned them
in skull for a new
set of eyes.

The bodega lights flickered
then banged black into the night.
It opened its eyes and cleared
out the crust by finger.
We are the blue rust
caught by flagpole.

And I saw them,
vampirites,
igniting cigarettes
under fluorescent
lights that
glared to their lottos
pressed between palm
and quarter.
I handed them
a single dollar
and entered,
the doormen
still outside,
scratching
and scratching
and scratching;

and they move their quarters,
planchettes across Ouija
lotto tickets, waiting
for the board to spell out
jackpot before sunrise.

Gone Gone

The mind is a wreck of a junkyard—
the static between radio stations.
In the car, I wipe the windshield frost
by sweatshirt sleeve, reach for
the radio knob.

Snowdrops flur in a still past the headlights,
my foot like a pepper grinder twisting against
the pedal. I'm too heavy on the throttle,
spinning tires, chucking slush.

Even the Air between Us

I won't ramble with specifics,

     first she sparked, then buried
back a word in her throat, lodged
in there, with bare fingers front lip
        knuckle forced.

     You were both in college. Experiences.
The kind you don't tell, but wave an arm
off the side of the embankment at you, glum soaked,
still,
     heels to ravine, a drive-by with no bullets
between airs, backward sunk under horizons.

Then, many nights, her morning
          and your mourning were carved
into tree trunks, both of you frozen
     ice block pillowcases, my ear resting,
        your mouths crystalized
     in blue.

     You walk
     guilt with shadow,
     bones with a leash,
my friend, how you
        tucked to the grody corners of the room,
lies running longitude lines
     over your invisible globe,
        you still run that latitude smile,
local music shows, wedding photos,

all the places you would go, I wasn't there ten years ago
but I saw everything.
          Even the air between us is glass, dare me
to slip through sill, bandit your mind, mug you,
               expose you,
                         give it up already nobody's buying.

She's been caught in the base of a snow globe
               that you shake once a year.

Tea bag conversations with a side of games,
          letter cubes from Scrabble pouches,
                         emptied and placed,
reached for your eyes,
               over a board between us,
          forgetting the spells and spellings of certain words,
Tell me, how do you spell this?

Peach Pit Stuck in a Lunar Phase

November sat shotgun,
car idled in the driveway
all winter long dropped
lit cigarettes out the window
into a tiny ash mountain
topped with a cherry stem.

I left her with a peach pit
like a parent moon
packed in my pocket,
stepped on the gas,
watched the tires
burn black against
the road that tracked us
North, smoke that formed
gray angels out the tailpipe.

I wanted to turn my
pockets inside out,
watch the gathered
pits rise like suede
moons above a market,
that orbit: pulling tides,
calling wolves.

Coup de Grace

I collect as bronze and bone[1],
kings and queens[2]
cemetery[3]
moans[4]

[1]: in a cross eyed copse / corpse dried / tossing shoveled mounds of dirt awry, / bullet in my back spilling / time and mud, this night grins yellow / with plaque and bone. / I'm sorry. / I wanted to make mom / proud, made my bed of dirt / before sleeping, now you won't / have to worry. Child,

[2]: of our legacies will rise / with bronze and bone, the

[3]: quakes, / seahorses of the soil with human hands / armed rifles, barrel pointing / your chest pops cold / of two winters / filling graves at our feet, / Hell's vents, / clogged with stone and bone,

[4]: and mouths filled with soil / sometimes you are the seeds / sometimes the rain we / talk in rectangles under a barrel.

A Grayscale Martyrdom

Marijuana passed like a laundry line
between the scattered party dwellers
connected in smoke. They settled behind
the orange glow of lighters where they
detached like jigsaw puzzles floating
in a bathtub.

The apartment cracked cold
and fractured itself into a seraph's
front shirt pocket.

I wasn't there to judge, I was there
to watch. Midnight never kissed
my cheek before, and I wanted to
know what it would be to make
the first move.

We squeezed through
the bathroom door at the same time:
Go ahead, no, you, no, no, I insist.

I wanted to lay my palms against
his cheekbones, suck his lips.

We gathered in a semicircle,
the tiles of the kitchen checkered
black and white maps beneath
us.

I felt stereotyped by the grayscale
shades of our souls, we shared
the silence in our pockets like
pinched mouths on the front
line of a martyrdom. The seraph
filled the gap, my fingers shone
like the muzzle flash of a rifle

when I met his hand with mine.
We laughed wild at his fingertips,
that blossomed into moonflowers.

My Father's Heirlooms

i.

Let's have a sleepover   that never ends,
          pillow wrap our heads,
deafen the shouting mouths
               carrying their sound
in time capsules
from elementary school.
          They parade the bedroom with picket signs
and loud colors reading
It's not over.

i.

Climb up to the top bunk
          take this,
you won't need it,
               it's been passed down
          from father
only you were born
with it. I was too;
it won't leave.

i.

Let's break ourselves in two
like wishbones,
          only,
I'll let you be   the bigger half, become
real and welcomed,
          I'll fade, and ignite
newspaper cones in gas doors
as a boy
ten years earlier.

Hole

The large ditch sunk centered,
young with dead leaves
in the woods, whenever
we arrived on those Friday nights
that wrapped our throats
like wool scarves.
The hole filled with junk
we carried with us—
empty beer cans, cigarette filters,
dime bags, blunt guts,
failed coursework, truth
or dares, Mom-kicked-me-out-
agains, makeouts, I-don't-want-to-
go-home-tonights.
Our trash can,
our bedroom,
and the graveyard
we surrounded.
I saw myself from the wind's perspective,
coming down like something heavenly, crashing
through the clouds, and diving into those woods,
passing through the treetops, separating myself
as I pushed through the tree limbs, butter pressed
through chain-linked fences, and reconnected
to myself on the other end, to see
a gathering of teenagers
encompassing a hole.
By Sunday The Pit cleared.
I'd imagine a man shaped
like a voodoo doll entering
those woods with a yarn-tangled
beard collecting remnants left
for The Pit, discovering the type
of people we once were.

Toy Chest

Soft with a silent hinge and heavy lift,
      my young arms discover
           a red ball in my chest, bleeding
      on porcelain hands,

I have not wined my delights yet dear mother,
                nor stained my front teeth red

instead I slap the colors of a Simon game lighting red
beating blue, like a pair of lungs broken in two.

How far does this go before it dries up?
Taking all these hits,
all the blows to my chest,
coughing out the feathers.

It's all gone. Packed away into a toy box now,
mother, you, the organizer of these antiques
                that pulse with phlegm and plush
with a voice as pink as wilted snapdragons.

From Grasshopper.

Some arms are gray,
or still green on the bank of a pond,
my leap from this fever dream
has drifted through town for ninety days.
If that warrants my return,
I'd love to have you again.

Lampposts on the block have
sprouted up like black tree trunks
strapped with cobwebbed handguns
stressed, and that lamppost,
once squandered by the swing
of a song in jest,
was the jump.

I am still the grasshopper.
Some legs are broke,
yet we trace this corpse
with chalk and road,
if only she tracked my song,
mason-jarred me, ignored
the hoots of owls and shelved me,
maybe she and I could grow together,
but, no, I was taken as host,
pregnant with you without consent,
maybe this watery grave will remain
uninvestigated under the scowls
of bad moons for days and days.

In Days

You have been stuck
between the paddles
of pinball machines.
Watched wedding
tapes inside a saran
wrapped bedroom,
volume on mute,
spoke over the tapes,
rewrote the manuscript
of our lives, letting
the calendar boxes
bind you to a bedpost.

I tried to scratch
an x over you like
a used date.
I, like the stray
cat we found caught
in a ball net—junked
in the backyard—you,
the one slipping gloves
over his hands, reaching—
we, became the twist and claw
dance of coercion.

Something tells me
you have been trying
to dig in the bedroom,
discover how deep
the roots of our mountains
really go.

But our bedroom
is not a mountainscape.

The dates on the calendar
surrounded our home
one day at a time, lighting
the house with the touch
of a torch.

I dug myself
into a casket encumbered
in soil, felt the heat
of woodland fire cultivations,
just a few more weeks,
until I blossom back.

Two Angels in a Body of a Thousand Colors

Car seat head rested ourselves inside passenger
windows, spot lit drifters along sidewalks,
found the first upright body complete with
two angels topped and bottomed out like
spinning plates in opposite directions. We
told one there's something caustic about Paris.

Only, this isn't Paris, I've never been there,
only the ride from the boat and back again,
saving the action from postcards and keychains
hung out front bodega corners on that shore,
this shore, paper clipped and dangled them
to my mind and maybe back to hers too.

From the lips, words poured out over herself
like a knotted chain of handkerchiefs and we
climbed down from the bedroom window
of her nostrils until we hit the ground, drove
off leaving behind the thousand colors spilling
pools of red, blue, pine, blue again, smeared
in rearview mirrors like brush strokes on glass
striking the reflection of my eyes and her own
from behind us as we stretched thin the gap
like taffy between back bumper, tire, and
languid angels dressed in moth eaten garb.

In Blur

I want to drink the tangled
red wine that pours from out
the foxhole of her mouth,
past her teeth and down
the moun-
            tain-
                  scape
at the midnight diner bar,
South shore, off the parkway,
paired with miniature whiskeys
spilling into my hot, green tea.
Her name tag comes close,
each letter spread into mosaic,
There's this memory I have
of you, Joselin
where you set
the teacup down,
walk out in blur.
She poured me another:
hot water and a teabag.
There's this dream I have
of you, Joselin. You
are in a picnic pattern
sundress, lead me to
a garden, and stick
the barrel of a gun in
my mouth.
You smile, and I melt
like a mangled bicycle
thrown to railroad tracks.
Gray double doors swing
forward, and backward.
Her shadow drags
like a cigarette
from behind the glass.

Casket Parts Hereafter

You researched casket parts nomenclature on the internet,
just so you can weave me a sweater from the overlay skirt

of coffins. We went mudding in St. Louis on our hands
and knees, leaving wet footprints on the sidewalks

tracking all the way back to Grasmere. We walked all about
the overpasses. We danced on the guardrails and spat

at the cars that passed under in coats of blur. Sometimes
we would catch each other's eyes through the reflection of sewage

water puddles. I would pack the Earl Grey tea bags and you
would get your hair caught in the barbed-wire tree branches

that surrounded the clearing in the woods. I am tired of replaying
your memories on the Super-8 tapes. You once told me

my words would come back to haunt me. I saw my words rise
from out the casket, shove their fist from out the grave mound,

limp across the field and pound against my cellar door.
They wrote themselves in claw marks dug throughout the wood.

That's not our wedding song you hear, it's our séance.

Nocturne

Like slipping on a silver nightgown
and leaning against the moonlit bark of a tree,
we lie as werewolf and bullet.

It's Wednesday again. It's been Wednesday
all week, it circles back,
to days we spend, have spent,
are spending the last
of, through gaps of vinyl blinds
laying in rays on the sofa.

So far, things have been silent. You sip your tea,
bruise a book to your lap, i wait for the moon;
To rise through my pupils.
You've pulled this trigger before.

It's Wednesday again,
as if it's some kind of heartbeat we can stake.
I know you can still see the confession booth
i've kept myself in, so slip into your silver
nightgown and spoon me with moonbeams.

Aerospace Web

Tractor wheels pressed their tire prints
to my sternum,
They mud and moat me,
But I want you to sculpt me
with sandcastles
by bucket
complete my city of sand
with little doors, toothpick flags,
hand on the sand knob,
twist, push, come
right in you angel
of the trenches
and dowel, you, reader,
filthy reader, the architect
of my supernova.

Find me frozen in lighthouse spotlights.
A child plays long division
with my eyebrows.
How many dollops of seaweed
will we leave behind when we
return turtle-like to the tides?

A conspiracy of ravens soars
in thermal pockets above my
mind, submerge yourself
to the ocean, again,
and again, and again.

Passersby in the Trainyard

the tallied moments lost between each blink becomes
the drifter   the circling tourist atop a platform their
thumb out   nursing maps   maybe caught on a stairwell
   in bedrooms   sometimes fornicated   throughout
door frames   passing through subway station turnstiles
between the train cars   maybe all the way up to
the moon   a moon that blinks between the turn of each
month   within each moon blink   rain   under rain
i become a boy kicking doorknobs down the avenue
i collect the fleeting junk caught above the grates
a drainpipe guarding the basin   of mutually collected
throwaways   caged ceilings for sidewalks   after
everything has passed   I slip under there with the crocodiles
   fashion gauntlets   from the teeth of ex-lovers
blinked   i banquo into the dinner parties   blink slept
throughout the turnstile moon cycle   finger in pocket
   pulled it out like a pocket watch and when you asked me
which train to take to get to the city   you asked me between
all the blinks   all the eyes all the eyes all the eyes
   i blinked in your eyes   for the first time

Last Words as a Love Letter

Loosen your fist, let the ice memorialize
   the water, fall backwards through a well pit
       with a quarter splash and echo.

With gin in hand
   the kaleidoscope spin of sobriety swallows
       you whole.

           I wasn't sure if you were floating in the Hudson,
or if the Hudson was floating in you.
   I tasted your knuckle tips as ghost prints

           on my lips, swam back to the   West
   shore in a glass bottle carrying a penciled
       message.

You slip your hand between
           the gap of my rib cage, floss the bone until it breaks,

           I'll take those punches to the gut now.

With Thanks

Thank you to all my friends and family for the support over the years. Thank you to my future wife, Veronica, for reading and rereading nearly all of these poems in every stage. Thank you to Liz at the deli for my 'usual' that kept me going during quarantine mornings.

Alec Montalvo is an English teacher and poet. He holds his Bachelors and MFA in Creative Writing with a focus in Poetry. He has been featured in magazines such as Manhattanville's Inkwell Journal, was a finalist in the Kallisto Gaia Press Contemporary Poetry Chapbook Competition, and holds publications in many small presses. In his spare time, Alec enjoys quality time with his tripod cat, Caulfield and playing tabletop games. Visit *Alecintheink.com* or *@Alecintheink* on Instagram.

Alec was born in Staten Island, New York, and received his Undergraduate Degree with Honors in Creative Writing with a focus in Poetry in 2014 from CUNY The College of Staten Island. Following, Alec began his education career teaching High school English in downtown Brooklyn for the NYC Department of Education. During this time, Alec also played Guitar in a local indie-rock band.

In 2017, Alec enrolled in Southern New Hampshire University's MFA program for Creative Writing. During this time, Alec began to construct his first collection of poetry and build his publication portfolio. Alec's poetry is inspired by magic-realism subgenres and he pulls influence from contemporary writers, fantasy fiction, and music. As of 2022, Alec continues to work for the NYC department of Education, teaching 8th grade English. He continues to write poetry and play guitar in his spare time. Follow his Instagram *@Alecintheink* or visit *Alecintheink.com* for inquiries, updates, and readings.

www.ingramcontent.com/pod-product-compliance
Lightning Source LLC
Chambersburg PA
CBHW022058080426
42734CB00009B/1402